Ancilla

Ancilla

Erin Murphy

LAMAR UNIVERSITY Press

ISBN: 978-0-9850838-5-4
Library of Congress Control Number: 2013954499

Cover Design: Diane Landskroener
X-ray image on front cover: by Wilhelm Röntgen in 1896
Book Design: Amy Morgan
Photo of author: Molly De Prospo
Manufactured in the United States

Lamar University Press
Beaumont, Texas

For my mother, Donna Murphy

Poetry from Lamar University Press

Alan Berecka, *With Our Baggage*
David Bowles, *Flower, Song, Dance*: Aztec *and Mayan Poetry* (a new translation)
Jeffrey DeLotto, *Voices Writ in Sand*
Mimi Ferebee, *Wildfires and Atmospheric Memories*
Ken Hada, *Margaritas and Redfish*
Michelle Hartman, *Disenchanted and Disgruntled*
Janet McCann, *The Crone at the Casino*
Dave Oliphant, *The Pilgrimage, Selected Poems: 1962-2012*
Carol Reposa, *Underground Musicians*

For information on these and other Lamar Press books go to
www.LamarUniversityPress.Org

Other Books by Erin Murphy

Distant Glitter
Word Problems
Dislocation and Other Theories
Science of Desire
Making Poems
Too Much of This World
For more information go to www.erin-murphy.com

Acknowledgments

North American Review
Southern Indiana Review
Nimrod International Journal
Kalliope
Atlanta Review
Beltway
Pennsylvania English
Interface
Dislocate
The Blue Max Review

"Mother of Invention" won the 2013 Fermoy International Poetry Competition.

Thank you to the Institute for Arts and Humanities at Penn State University, the Penn State Altoona Advisory Board, and the Virginia Center for Creative Arts for time and funding to complete this project.

Special thanks to the following early readers of this manuscript: Belle Hollon, Dinty W. Moore, Richard De Prospo, Susan Kan, Todd Davis, Donna Murphy, Meredith Davies Hadaway, Julia Spicher Kasdorf, and Julianna Baggott. Thank you also to Gene Barry, Jerry Craven, Noel King, Lori Bechtel-Wherry, Kenneth Womack, and Brian Black.

Ancilla [Latin]: maidservant, root of ancillary

[S]ex is but the ancilla of art.

—from *Lolita* by Vladimir Nabokov

CONTENTS

I.

II.

III.

I.

Hand Mit Ringen

I have seen my death!

—Anna Bertha Röntgen, upon seeing her
hand captured by her husband, Wilhelm,
in the first x-ray

At first you were no different
from the others who frequented
my father's café. Some came

for food and drink; others called
upon Papa to translate their essays
into Latin. But you, it seemed,

had other designs. Your eyes cut
through the bar's din and clatter
to meet mine. When I gave you

my hand, I never meant it
literally, and yet there it is,
ring and all, immortalized

in a bony bon voyage. I still
remember that winter evening
in your lab, the heartbeat of

the grandfather clock, wires
and bulbous tubes, the window
a photograph of skeletal trees.

Your colleagues said we'd be
in high fortune if you'd patent
your findings. But you were

never one to take credit.
At the Nobel ceremony, you
slipped out the back door before

they called you to the stage. Nor
did you ever assign blame. I love
the story of your classmate

chalking a caricature of the teacher
on the heating stove. Refusing
to reveal his name, you were

sent out into the cold with no hope
for a degree. But you showed them
all and did what you had to do.

Dear Wilhelm, we have everything
but time. And I don't need an x-ray
to see what's inside of you.

Vienna Legends

The only story of Beethoven's reported meeting
with Mozart was told by a boy named Ignaz
Seyfried who went on to become a composer.

When I think back to that spring afternoon,
I'm not sure if the parlor was filled with sunlit dust

or if it's my memory that glints and flits.
Ludwig, a wiry boy, arrived first, ran his hand

along the keys. He asked my age and said he'd had
as many years when he'd quit school. I'd wager he said it

with regret, though he seemed to prefer studying
the floor to reading books or even a fellow's face.

At any rate, soon Mozart and the others came
and took their seats as if the very chairs

were made for them alone. Even then, shoulder high,
I thought it takes a certain kind of man to think

of every surface as a throne. Ludwig performed.
My eye on law, not music, I cannot tell you what

I heard, but I'll not forget what Mozart said:
With such preparation, that piece could be performed

as well by anyone. Even by this boy here, he said,
and motioned to me in the corner where I did my best

to disappear. Ludwig shifted on his bench,
then asked, *Please then, sir, would you be so kind*

as to suggest a theme? Mozart complied, tossed a tiny bone
to a hungry dog, then sat back, arms afold, and gave his

companions a sideways glance. I did not yet know music,
but I knew this: Ludwig improvised the way one recalls

a fevered dream, each note leading to the next as if they
played his hands rather than the other way 'round.

From Mozart's brow, all wrinkles fell. His skin
became as smooth as the Alpengarten skating pond.

And when he took young Ludwig's hand in his
and, full voice, pronounced, *Mark that young man;*

he will make himself a name in the world, you will see,
I pretended, I must confess, his words were meant for me.

Alma Mahler, Postnuptial

A husband and wife who are both composers:
how do you envisage that? If, at a time when you
should be attending to household duties or
fetching me something I urgently needed...if at
such a moment you were befallen by
'inspiration': what then? From now on you have
only one profession: to make me happy!
—Gustav Mahler to Alma before they married

Gustav, I composed
myself and became your

bride, swallowing scores
that lay inside me, waiting

to be born. I learned to play
the scales of others'

desires—first yours,
then our daughters',

their cries like crystal
chimes. Yet even

that role wasn't mine
to keep. When little Maria

fell ill, color rushing
from flushed cheeks,

you turned within. And I—
I turned to other men.

What could have been
a feud became, instead,

a fugue. I've given up
my music. I've given up

my name. You treat me
as you treat your

orchestra: like a lion
that must be tamed.

Kant's Manservant

Marriage is the reciprocal use of
each other's sexual organs.
—Immanuel Kant

Sir, a confession: the beef I served
at mealtime today was cut from a cow
killed in anger, not lulled to death

as you prefer. And I was the one
who urged Jachmann to join you
on your walk along the linden trees,

defying boldly your fear of speaking
in open air. It all comes back
to the gold jacket, the one you'd

have me sell, its hue too close
to the sun. Forgive me, sir, but you
could use a little color. The walls,

bare but for the muted engraving
of Rousseau, are blank as the page
you face at your desk each dawn,

bent bird in a nightcap and gown,
still stiff from my pressing.
Sir, what moves you? They would have

married you, both ladies, had you not
stayed so long in the dark room
of your mind. Ending a meal in laughter

will urge your bowels along but won't
bleach your life of desire. Know this:
I will wear the jacket for my wedding, sir,

for my bride-in-waiting who will be
beautiful, simply, objectively beautiful,
dancing the ländler, tucking a yellow curl

behind her ear. And you will grant me
leave for the afternoon. Yes, you will
grant me leave with pay, so that

years from now I will be here
to pour you a pint of claret, to collect
the scattered crumbs that are your words.

Nietzsche's Sister

Man shall be educated for war
and woman for the recreation of the warrior.
—Friedrich Nietzsche

A nurse, Friedrich.
You were a nurse
in the war, a nurse
with no stomach

for blood. As for
the war of the mind,
let's not forget
whose has gone soft

as our father's:
they found you
plowing the piano
with your elbows,

and before that,
on your knees,
embracing a mare
in the streets of Turin.

Tell me, brother:
if a young girl cries
and no one listens,
does she make

a sound? Not in a house
brimming with women
who serve a boy
named for a king.

When your palm
was scorched from
the batch of matches
you lit to prove

a schoolyard point,
I cried for you.
But now my tears
are a puzzle.

Are we not happy,
you ask, *Are we not?*
It was a *we*
I wanted when I ran

to Bernhard,
to everything you
loathed. You
called me *llama*

and I dipped this
bitterness in honey
and played the part
of mascot. But I

know the likeness
you drew: a llama
sprays spittle
at its rival, coughs

its own fodder
to keep the fight.
Now, with your
right side limp

as the wool britches
mother mended
for you in the evenings,
mark these words:

I will scream
and stomp and kick
and cough and spit:
I will make noise.

Serving Schopenhauer

We set the clock at Englischer Hof
by his face, more sour than the sauerbraten
Herr ordered each evening. And the gold coin—
such an odd ritual: on the edge of the table
during dinner, back in his left pocket after.

Good paying customer, tallies his tip
to the pfennig, I was told on hire,
then warned: *Don't speak unless spoken to.*
I vowed silence, for my children at home,
for the new one coming, for my wife
who was still weak from birthing.

Everyone knew his father had left
this world by his own hand,
that his mother had pushed him—
her own son!—
from the second floor.
For years his body kept moving
long after his spirit had died.

Then one morning, emptying the garbage
out back, I saw him walking a poodle
in the alleyway. The dog whimpered
and Herr lifted her gently, examined
her paw, kissed it. *Atma*, he said,
Poor, poor Atma.

That night I asked him about the coin.
I will drop it in the poor box,
he snorted, *when I hear talk of anything*
besides horses, women, or dogs.
Thinking not of my earnings, I asked,
Do you not have words for Atma?

His fork chattered to the floor
like a child's toy tossed down a stairwell.
When he looked at me I saw
a flicker of fear. Yes, it's true:
between one and none there lies an infinity.
If he had counted thoughts that day,
many hungry children would have eaten.

Basho’s Disciple Challenges the Master to a Haiki no Renga

your banana tree
and thatched hut, your raging heart:
fire outside and in

    under light of the eighth moon
    I left without provisions

you walked away from
what you knew and toward some
shrouded future self

    mount fuji was erased by
    morning fog, hovering clouds

you took your name from
a tree, yet you are a frond
in the autumn wind

    bashos are known to thrive when
    transplanted, liberated

you have hardened like
bamboo dipped in stiff laquer,
it—you—will not bend

I'm a half-opened lotus,
a hand giving, accepting

if you look too far
ahead you might trip over
your own pine tree roots

I sleep among miscanthus
and bush clover tapestries

you lift your lantern
to alight the road ahead,
obscuring your face

clothed in darkness and shadows,
I am illuminated

your bowl is upturned,
a thick film of dust gathers
in your cooking pot

my gourd overflows with rice
my cup is filled with sake

your father aspired
to be a high samurai,
left this life—and you

my office was the forest
I answered to the seasons

you were a lost boy
abandoned, cold, and cleaving,
hungry for a crumb

> child squatting by the river,
> I tossed him food from my sleeve

wood cut in the west
echoes, echoes in the east
to those who listen

> koya is dotted with monks,
> bare lodgings and bare longings

the sinking sun is
your companion in sadness,
your one loyal friend

> you don't fret about robbers
> when your pockets are empty

haikai no renga
would not exist without two
poets and two pens

> bleached white cloth stretched out to dry:
> blank as paper, as my mind

I know a village
woman who would bow her head,
offer you her heart

oh, unfurled red star lily,
oh, skylark piercing the blue

you latched the door to
the world only to have it
howl like a stray dog

then came lightness—*karumi*—
and I embraced the mundane

what you cannot move
can move you if you sit still:
a boulder, desire

I have wanted and wanted
not to want what is not mine

Jane Austen's Letters to Sister Cassandra, Abridged

January 1796

I was nice.

I behaved.

But love

was cut-up

silk gloves

and old paper

hats. Regret

is a vessel,

not a spinning-wheel.

The wind proved

to be my

future, delivered it

to me with

a sigh. I flirt

with tears.

I write.

The Other Daughter

Mary Wollstonecraft's first child addresses her mother

They knew there was trouble
when the doctor brought puppies
to your breasts to draw milk.

Stroke the cat. Play with the dog.
Eat the bread. Drink the milk.

I was a shadow in the hall,
half-sister, step-child to a man
whose indifference stung
more than hate.

Lay down the knife. Look at the fly.
See the horse. Shut the door.

In the years since the baby
named for you took your place,
I have grown less sure
about Scandinavia, about
whether the memories are mine
or yours, preserved now
on the study shelf with your lessons.

Get your book. Hide your face.
Wipe your nose. Wash your hands.

I still taste the herring,
still see the Swede servants
washing linen in the winter sea,
their hands, cut by ice,
cracked and bleeding.

Why do you cry? Shake hands.
I love you. Kiss me now. Good girl.

It must have been cold,
but I found warmth
in the curve of your neck,
those days before the laudanum,
before the jump from Putney Bridge,
before the midwife and the whispers
and the closed doors, before I had to live
with this girl, hungry as ivy,
always clawing her way elsewhere.

The bird sings. The fire burns.
The cat jumps. The dog runs.

You named me for your friend
who died giving birth.
O, so many parallels, so many
lives running side by side
toward different destinations!

The bird flies. The cow lies down.
The man laughs. The child cries.

I love you, mother.
Kiss me now.
The child dies.

The Fall

> *"[Mother] lay there unable to help herself for a long time, neither calling out nor able to reach her bell rope or so much as a shoe to make a noise with, and wake us in the next room."*
>
> —Ralph Waldo Emerson

It was William who showed
promise as a scholar,
Charles a close second
with his Latin Prize.

Edward was by far most
charming; his hair had
a life of its own. All
are gone now—Charles

to consumption,
Edward to madness,
then to his grave,
and William to the days

of an ordinary working man.
Yet you, dear Waldo, seemed
the ordinary one in youth:
chubby and middling

in matters of the mind.
Even your birth was
unremarkable: your father,
home from Election Day,

noted your arrival
the way a cook takes stock
of the pantry. He kissed
my forehead, then retreated

to his study to compose
Sunday's sermon.
He was a rigid man,
or at least wished to be

known as such. At the top
of each hour he moved
to the next item in his routine:
reading practical authors,

sermonizing, studying scripture.
What a departure from
my own father, who strode
down the aisle at Trinity Episcopal

in his red cloak, wielding
his hat underarm like a rifle.
Even the air, it seemed,
distilled in his presence.

The nearest display of pageantry
you witnessed was your father's
procession to King's Chapel
burying ground. With the coaches

and artillery company,
there was no time for tears.
But no matter: you had
sewn yourself a pocket

for your sorrow years before
there was reason. It stretched
to hold your brother, lost
when he was only a boy,

your beloved Helen,
and your own Waldo, just 5.
I've buried enough of my own
to know there is a point

when you wait for grief's seizure
to rattle you in its grasp,
yet it does not come. All of this
I feel but cannot say,

any more than I can tell you
I did not fall from the bed
but thrust myself upon
the hard wood floor.

A bad dream, you assumed.
But truth be told,
there is only so long
that we can drift about

like fickle snowflakes
in the Concord wind,
uncertain where we will land
or with whom.

Cleaning 328 Mickle Street

Since you was here, Alma, I have had
a friend move in, Mrs. Davis, strong & hearty
& good natured, a widow, young enough,
furnishes me my meals & takes good care.
—Walt Whitman in a letter to Mrs. Alma Johnston, March 4, 1885

It was not for marriage
that I moved in with you,
Mr. Whitman, and not for
peace & quiet, either: the trains
from Camden and factory whistles
rival only the "Star Spangled Banner"
bellowed from your bath.
It was for no such proposal
that I turned a shoulder
to the church ladies sneering
at market as I handpicked
a bucket of full-bellied oysters
for your supper and chose
the beans for your twice-brewed
coffee, thick as the stench
of guano drifting across the Delaware.

I needed not a man but a sturdy
mantle to hold the remnants
of my former life: my husband's
wool sailing cap, the compass

from his maiden ship, thrown off now
from true direction. You'd have me
think you're a sailor yourself
with your *damns* and *hells*
and orders to *ram a needle*
up the bookbinder's *ass*.
But I've been close enough
to smell your soap and cologne.
I've filled the bowl by your chair
with mignonette and roses and lilacs,
at your request. And I've seen you
save my lacework shirts
for reading your Mr. Lincoln poem.

We've had our fun:
when *Mr. Trouble*, as I call him,
knocks, I ring the bell three times
as warning. And we laugh
about your room, more full of dust
than Mickle Street after a whorl
comes rolling through. It's safe
to tell you now I only
got a broom in there on days
you took to town in your buggy
pulled by that stiff-kneed pony,
and even then I had to wade
through notes and receipts,
billheads and letters and proofs
and scraps of wallpaper saved
for who knows what. Your life spilled

from that iron-banded double-hasped trunk,
as massive in its own way
as this stone tomb, as the man
you aimed to be.

The Lost Letter

I took pleasure in taking care of her—she thought everything of me—when any thing went wrong she would come to me.
—Lavinia Norcross, aunt of Emily Dickinson

I've failed at my primary employment—
being a person, you said when last you wrote.
Dearest Emily, you've failed only
at not knowing in what you shine. A person
is not simply one who, like your sister,
dusts the stairs and busies herself
with pussies and posies. Young men
may fancy playing spooney with Vinnie,
but with you they wish to talk late into the evening,
after other less spiritual souls have
buried themselves in feather pillows.

Remember the thunderstorm on the way
to Monson, just after we passed Mr. Clapps' place?
You were not quite three, yet you
bellowed *the fire! the fire!*— your first
attempt at poetry. Now you send me such lines as
Oh if remembering were forgetting.
That visit you plucked away at the piano,
calling it *moosic*, the same name you gave
to the songs of the cows at Dillingsworth Dairy.
After you left I found your tiny red apron
by the hearth and used it as a handkerchief

as I wept and wept. You were my child
before my children, and tho I'd never
tell Loo or Fanny, I felt I'd nearly used up
my best love before they came.
Yes, if remembering were forgetting.

Em, dear, I am not well, as I'm sure Vinnie reported
after her visit. She was a perfect nurse,
boiling and scrubbing and fluffing through the week.
But now the simple task of taking air
is the hard work of a fieldhand, and even as I
write this I must pause with my pen
as if summoning great thoughts. No,
that is *your* primary employment. Please
remember not to forget it.

Poe's Last Letter, Abridged

—from Edgar Allan Poe's letter to Maria Clemm

Love is

nothing

[nothing]

but fear

with a name

& address.

I will marry

[marry]

my own

[own]

death.

13 Ways of Looking at Wallace Stevens

I.
Daughter Holly reads "A Child Asleep in its Own Life"

The red convertible
on my 16th birthday—
that was for me.
But this poem? No.
Not for me, not for
any child but for
the part of you
that is not too old
to see the world
as new.

II.
The Ice Cream Manufacturer's Association
responds to "The Emperor of Ice Cream"

Mr. Stevens, please clarify:
are you for ice cream
or against it?

III.
Bride in Hartford, Described by Stevens
as "the genius of poetry...out of place,"
Turns to Her Mother During the Photo Shoot

Mother, please do something about that odd
man who keeps staring at me. He gives me the willies.

IV.
Response to an English Philosopher of Great Distinction Who Has Asked if He May Call on Stevens at His Office

No.

V.
Request from the Key West Visitors' Bureau

In place of order, might we suggest *beauty, tranquility, peacefulness, perfection, wonder,* or *harmony*?

VI.
A Group of Students Sneaks Out During Stevens' Harvard Reading

The shuffle of shoes
and coats and books,
the squeaky yawn of doors,
the poet announcing
the title of his next poem:
"As You Leave the Room."

VII.
Critic Louis Renza Responds to "The Emperor of Ice Cream"

"Cigar as 'corona' both puns on 'coroner' and doubles as a metonym for a 'crown,' although not exactly of an emperor. Crown equally doubles as a vulgar idiomatic allusion to the head of a penis [needless to say, 'corona' and 'crown' are not in the text]. Calling 'the roller of big cigars' thus means invoking the biologistic force that results in erections, which, as 'the muscular one,' the roller personifies. And just as one prepares food to satisfy physical appetites, his whipping up 'concupiscent curds' in 'kitchen cups' evokes filling testicles with sperm, the goal of which is sheer pleasurable discharge for the male."

VIII.
Postcard to His Wife, Elsie, from Bethlehem, Pa.

Pictured on front: *Moravian Funeral of the Olden Times*
Scribbled on back: *The local idea of a good time. Love, Wallace*

IX.
Elsie Greets the Mt. Holyoke Faculty
Who Will Escort Stevens to His Lecture

What do you teach? My ancestors were concerned with education. What's that, dear? Do I need to go into that now? No, I suppose not. I never went to college, but I made good marks, and I got an A in composition in the 4th grade. I made you some cocoa and biscuits. Wallace says the biscuits are too dry, but like I say, it's the nature of biscuits to be dry, don't you agree? My ancestors were Swiss schoolmasters, the first schoolmasters in Berks County...oh, I'm sorry, Wallace doesn't like for me to talk about myself. But I do like people to know that I'm interested in something besides cooking and cleaning. Oh dear, you haven't finished your cocoa!

X.
Joe Poet, M.F.A., Takes a Job at MetLife

How the hell did he do it?

XI.
Poet Catherine Field Explores
Stevens' Secretary's Point of View

Did she blush to write "Complacencies of the peignoir" in shorthand for that strange boss, wistful herself for those oranges and that coffee she might have had, had he chosen instead to have lunch?

XII.
Something Else His Secretary Might Have Considered

Words typed onto a blank page
are like scratch footprints of a tiny creature
that has stepped in ink
A blackbird, perhaps, walking in the snow

XIII.
Letter from His Mother

My father called making shoes
a leap of faith: the hope that heel and toe
have room but not too much.
You have not spoken to your father
since you took Elsie as your bride.
I will try not to pry. Perhaps the shoe
is not so different from the poem:
you stitch it, shape it, send it out
into the world like a child.

II.

The Virgin Queen Elizabeth I on the Spanish Armada, Abridged

I desire

loving.

Have my

heart,

my

heat.

Lay down,

honour my blood,

body.

Invade

my virtues,

my prince,

and you shall

have

my kingdom.

Dear Father

Martha Bryan was the daughter of Timothy Matlack, scrivener of the Declaration of Independence

Oh, how the Quakers would despise
Mr. Peale's portrait—your crimson
and powder-blue suit, that silk scarf,

the fine tablecloth and scattered books,
all of the accouterments of class at your
disposal. And yet: you are not one

to bow down at the throne of endowment
or rank. You fancy horses and cockfights,
did your time for debt, and have always

held that the darkest among us deserve
a white man's rights. I remember those
mornings I sat in your study, my legs

swinging from the straight-back chair
as I joined cursive characters like paper dolls.
It is self-evident, you would tease, *that all*

letters are created equal. Yet capitalizations
deserve their own flourishes. Note my
salutation: the *D* curls like the furled scroll

copy tucked away in your desk. As you
cupped my hand in yours, guiding it across
the page, we were a pair of skaters cutting ice.

You were known as a sword-toting patriot
back then. Nowadays, the only weapon
you wield is a pen.

The Pantomime's Progeny

[Deburau's Pierrot was a] figure pale as the moon, mysterious as silence, supple and mute as the serpent, long and straight as the gibbet.

—Charles Baudelaire on Jean-Gaspard Deburau, the pantomime known for his version of the Pierrot character.

You were not some bumbling
English clown stuffed with bloody

roast beef, barreling wing-to-wing
like a human hurricane.

You taught me wordlessly
that what we're not matters more

than what we are. You were a star.
You graced the stage in loose pants

and a billowing chemise, every bit
as lithe as your acrobatic family.

Required to enter with a stunt,
most mimes chose tightrope, a feat

mastered easily. But you came in
on your hands, seeing the world

as you preferred it: upside down,
like the wealthy patrons sitting

with the lower class, like the tears
you summoned alongside laughs.

Silence was the rule back then,
in shows and in our home.

The only sounds came from
your adoring crowds. Now that

you're gone and I have taken
your place, their silence is

unspeakably loud, louder than
the noon hour in the clockmaker's

shop where you forced me
to apprentice when I was young,

determined to set me on any path
but your own. Father, the rules

have changed. We can speak now
in our acts. Yet silence

is what I choose. It is who I am
and what I do. What I am not is you.

Gutenberg's Verdict, Abridged

—from "The Helmasperger Notarial Instrument"

Gutenberg:

brother, messenger,

priest,

master of

golden work.

Give him

faith

and parchment, paper,

ink!

[Gutenberg] O [Gutenberg]:

free these

and other

words.

To Nellie, with Love from the Letter E

She was considered the best reporter in America.
—*New York Evening Journal*'s editor
Arthur Brisbane on Elizabeth Cochrane,
(a.k.a. Nellie Bly), the first female
investigative reporter

For the silent e in Cochrane,
added to your surname to elevate
your status. E for the egging on

of your half-dozen brothers
who dared you to scale the tallest
apple tree and ride the old horse

on your feet. E for the education
on which your judge father insisted,
for the eligible bachelors your mother

paraded, afraid you'd become
a spinster—or worse—a schoolmarm.
E for Erasmus Wilson whose column

"What Girls Are Good For" inspired
your furious retort, for the editor who
hired his first lady reporter for $5 a week,

and for the errand boy who hummed
"Nelly Bly" while cleaning the cuspidor
as the newsroom staff lobbed possible

pennames: *Heigh, Nelly ho, Nelly*
listen lub to me,/I'll sing for you,
play for you, a dulcem melody.

E for your eagerness to read your first
published article that Sunday morning
in Uncle Thomas's parlor as the paper

sat unopened till well after services.
E for your enraged family who feared
this gently-reared cultured girl

would be sent off to the saloons.
E for the exasperation you felt
writing anonymous reviews

of choral society shows—and then,
for your escape to Mexico,
New York and finally, around

the globe in less than eighty days.
E for the experts who declared you
insane, sending you undercover

to Blackwell's Island. E for your exposé
on mental asylums where women were
fed moldy bread and forced to sleep

in rat-infested beds. E for your
searching eyes, grey with flecks of violet.
E for Elizabeth, no longer silent.

Calamity Jane at the Dime Museum

It's the showman's place to supply what the
public wants, if he can find out what that is.
—George Middleton, who hired Martha
Jane Canary Burke (a.k.a. Calamity Jane)
as an attraction in his dime museum

Never trust a man who starts believin'
his own lies, I always say. A woman,

though—that's another story. Miss Jane
could spin a yarn like she was knittin'

sweaters for every sucker who
dreamed of gold. We signed her for

fifty bucks a week and all expenses,
twice what the Fat Lady gets, 'less you

count Big Winny who broke the scales
and the bank. Two shows a day

Miss Jane gave us, and we gave her
top billing—"Scout, Trapper and

Indian Slayer"—which didn't sit too well
with the Aboriginal albino beauty

or Texas Jack, the one-armed whittler.
Even Ralston the Rattlesnake King

was sore, which took some nerve
since his rattlers were tamer than

a litter of purring kittens. But business
is business. And the cost of the costume

was hers to bear: $11 boots and who
knows how much for the buckskins

and the Winchester she cradled like a baby.
It's true she liked a nip...or three

or four, *partaking freely of that which*
leaveth color on the nose, as one reporter

wrote. But she weren't no trouble,
really—showed up on time and posed

for photos. We woulda kept her on
for another tour, but there was somethin'

told me she was a one-off act.
The people came and paid their dimes,

shuffled down the hall past fortune tellers
and typewritin' contests to the corner

where Miss Jane sat up on her stool.
What they'd heard about her back

in the day could fill a real museum,
but what they saw was a woman

with hair goin' gray and a mouth
that seems like it'd made up its mind.

She coulda been your teacher in
grade school or the lady sellin' feed

at the general store. You see, folks
have had enough of real life. They want

somethin' curious, somethin' shiny,
somethin' more.

Emma Lazarus's Statue of Liberty Sonnet, Abridged

The brazen,

mighty woman,

mother of

pomp

with lips

yearning to

refuse
our shore,

send these homeless

to the

door.

Pluck and Jive

> *[When I learned to play 'St. Louis Blues'], everything changed for me...I was on my own playing jazz music, for there are no rules in it for the harp to go by.*
>
> —Olivette Miller, harpist and daughter of comedian Flournoy Miller of the minstrel duo Miller and Lyles

Do you know how good you've gotta be
for white folks to think you're playing
a colored man? My daddy's routine

was so foolproof a dog could bark at it
and make you laugh. There he was,
a black man wearing blackface and a hat,

and when everyone was clapping
and slapping their knees, he'd peel off
a glove and wave a hand lighter

than their own. Still he had to use
the back door. 'Course the real ones
trying to pass were Amos & Andy

who ripped off my daddy's act
and waited a decade to throw him a bone:
scriptwriting consultant. Consultant!

Ha! That's like calling Joe Louis
an apprentice instead of a heavyweight.
Those years were rough for daddy,

though you wouldn't have known
unless you'd seen him at home,
his eyes dimming more each day.

He bought me my first harp, told me
not to listen too hard to the music outside
my own head, not to listen at all

to what other people said. Sometimes
I played more for him than me 'cause
when you can make your daddy smile,

it feels like a crime to do otherwise.
Truth be told, it was even worse when
he went to work for the show,

head bowed like he'd been scolded.
But what do I know? I only know
how to coax a melody outta thin air,

how to brace a harp between my legs
and rest the shoulder on my own.
The trick to looking ladylike is

a mile-high slit in your fitted skirt.
Gives the audience a glimpse of thigh,
a hint of what else you've got. You see,

holding a harp is like holding up
a man, something you do whether
he asks you to or not.

III.

Archimedes' Widow

Do not disturb my circles.
—the last words of Archimedes

In the public square they tell the tale
of your famous bath: how the water's

rise mirrored your size and mass.
Eureka! Eureka! you bellowed

to neighbors without bothering to drape
yourself in a robe. Or so the story goes.

Truth is, it was I who lowered myself
into the tub until it overflowed.

Bare and wet, I mopped the tiles.
Other men might have reached for me

but not you—your eyes burned
with thought. Oh, irregular flesh,

unwieldy tears! I know you wish
women were concepts to be learned

and taught. Some say, my dear,
that you forestalled the city's siege

with a single hand. Yes, a body displaces
water. And legend displaces a man.

Galileo's *Sidereal Messenger*, Abridged

With this instrument

of our
senses,

behold the moon,

naked and rough

as a philosopher wandering

in Paris or at sea.

Forsake

caution— let ABCD

be a cloud, a face,

a hand, the sun

as shadows lose

their blackness

and become one.

Mother of Invention

[My brother's] premature death left my parents disconsolate...Anything I did that was creditable merely caused my parents to feel their loss more keenly.

—Nikola Tesla, developer of the AC electrical supply system. His mother, Georgina-Djuka Tesla, invented her own household tools, including a mechanical eggbeater.

What's a horse in full stride
but alternating currents—
right legs, left legs, right:
a sharing of burdens.

You were only five
the year we lost Dane.
It nearly cost my mind,
but it's you who really paid.

I fear that in our grief,
we left you to the wind,
a freshly-wrung bed sheet
hung without a pin.

Thunder shook the room
the night that you were born.
Thunder shook my womb:
thunder, lightning, moan, moan.

The doctors called it sickness
when your senses went astray.
You could hear the *tick tick ticks*
of watches three rooms away

and visualize inventions whole
in a sudden mental flood
while I sketched out my tools
on butcher paper flecked with blood.

Thunder shook the room
the night that you unfurled.
Some said you came too soon,
but you were ready for the world.

As a boy, you'd take your bath
out in the sunny yard
and chase after Mačak,
stroking his fur to create sparks.

I can still see your popgun
fashioned from cornstalks,
see you leaping from the barn
with a lady's parasol.

Da-dum-da-dum-da-dum,
like the Marko epics I recall.
In electricity, too, there's rhythm—
in life: *da-dum...da...*

Thunder shook the room
the night that you arrived.
The midwife said child of storm.
but I saw a child of light.

The Causticity Principle

> *It's much easier to find one's way if one isn't too familiar with the magnificent unity of classical physics. You have a decided advantage there, but then lack of knowledge is no guarantee of success.*
>
> —Wolfgang Pauli to Werner Heisenberg

You played the part of scientist
as others paid their dues. You tramped

and camped the mountainsides
while I hunched over numbers

in a paneled room. What we know
is a wooden block, solid as a stern fist.

What we don't know is a sealed box
that rattles like a toy when shaken.

What we know we don't know
is the moment before we've fully

awakened, the blur between daylight
and dream. And then there is

what we don't know we don't know:
a cloud hovering above the horizon's

seam, this way a father's raised brow,
that way a question mark. Who?

Where? How? Why? I have spent
a lifetime feeling my way through

the dark while you charge head-first
with no reason, no rhyme.

Letter from Charles Darwin to Botanist Joseph Dalton Hooker, June 27, 1573, Abridged

The pretense that science is objective, apolitical and value-neutral is profoundly political because it obscures the political role that science and technology play in underwriting the existing distribution of power in society.

—Ruth Hubbard

My wife: like gales

of wind, less

and less endurable,

with highness and lowness,

eclectic & not clear.

Men, supreme, are

the highest

form, the most

mature, having important

organs & ideas.

Facing Manet

"M. Manet has exhibited a philosopher
trampling on oyster shells, and a water-colour
of his Christ supported by angels. The
[exhibition] Club should try harder."

—author Edmund Duranty in a Feb. 19,
1870 *Paris-Journal* review, which led,
four days later, to a fencing duel between
himself and his friend, Edouard Manet

Is it true a man's grievances
are heavier than his grief?
You should know, Edouard.
Your salon rejections weigh on you
more, it seems, than the memory
of Alexandre, your *boy with the cherries*,
hanging from the thin cord
in your studio attic, a stick
of barley sugar pressed between
his teeth.

A sculptor I once reviewed
told me this: to sculpt a bird
you start with a block of marble
and take away everything that isn't a bird.
O, if life were marble! I have chipped away
at the space my father should have filled
and found not a man but an angry child
clawing at the clouds. Your own son

limps along with another name
and calls you *godfather*. For shame.
This is not *light dancing on colour*, Eduoard.
This is a carpenter with shattered hands,
a cartographer who has lost his sight.

So, we will fight. We will meet at 11 a.m.
in the Forest of Saint-Germain.
You will wear shoes too generous in size,
bought just for this day. I can already
write the ending: we will collapse
in the grass, laughing, comrades again.
First, you will aim for my chest,
lancing flesh the way you scraped
the palette knife against your Christ's heart.
And you and I, who grip weapons
like a young girl fingers a spider
found creeping in her quarters, will lunge forth,
clumsy and dumb, the way men do in hate
and in love.

Love Poem to Michelangelo

...by the steep, long road
there is none who arrives, Lady,
unless you join humility and kindness;
the climb stiffens, my strength fades,
and I am breathless at halfway.
—Platonic poem written by Michelangelo
to friend Vittoria Colonna

All of Rome assumes your strength
wells from the way you chisel secrets
of solid marble. I know the truth:

your words lured me from the island
of sadness known only by women
whose husbands' eyes have turned to stone.

How I long to climb down
from the *lucente diadema*
on which you have placed me,

to reach deep within you the way
you say true artists reach for the *concetto*,
the soul-image. It could have happened

the day at the convent when you
sat across the tiled table, a sheaf
of sunlight at your feet. My years

with Francesco seemed then
a faint breeze, a memory you can't
distinguish from a dream. You wondered

if a humble sin means less to God
than a bounty of good. *Is this a sin*?
I wanted to ask, lifting the hair

from your neck and pressing my fingers
deep into the muscles that held
your head Heavenward as you worked

paint into the chapel's fresh plaster.
Or this? And here I would have
stroked your nose, curved since

Torrigiani's punch. To you, crooked;
to me, a sign that you have lived
among men, not above them.

Letter from Van Gogh to Émile Bernard, Abridged

December 1887, Letter 1

I live frightfully.

I'll not

behave.

There's desire.

And then there's

righteousness.

I see it

as a grave.

Origen de Las Dos Fridas

I must have been six years old when I had the intense experience of an imaginary friendship with a little girl.

—Frida Kahlo in her diary, 1950

When your family threw open the balconies
on La Calle de Allende, welcoming
wounded Zapatistas with corn gorditas—

When polio seized you in its grip
like a lover, shriveling your leg
to a whittled stick—

When the streetcar crushed your
spine and spirit, the handrail puncturing
your womb like a matador's sword—

When the doctor locked you inside
an orthopedic corset until you colored
your plaster cage with desire—

When Diego—*tu accidente sugundo*—
set you on fire and watched you burn till you
sought the kind of love he hadn't earned—

When—as a girl—you huffed your pane
of glass and drew a door to our world
where we danced beneath cedron trees—

I was there—hovering like a storm
cloud on canvas—real as your own gaze.

I was your father's vertigo—the strokes
that dulled your mother—your weakness
for a liter of aged tequila—your other.

I was the gold exploding from the artisan's
pouch in the crash—powder sooting
your blood as it seeped the streets.

I was each of the three blank pages
in your diary—and the entries you
yanked like hairs at the root.

I was the country you loved
to love—baroque and broken like
the body you gilded in ribbons and chains.

I was everything you ever wanted
a painting and a man to be:
beautifully brutal, brutally honest.

I was the jangling of your bulbous
jewels announcing your arrival in every
room like an omen—or a promise.

Postcards from Ghost Ranch

I suspect I'm a better chauffeur than writer.
—Maria Chabot, an aspiring writer who worked as a caretaker at Georgia O'Keefe's properties in New Mexico

1.
Frost clings to windows till noon.
Navajo Canyon lets loose
a gloriously wet sneeze of snow. And later,
bands of white lie in lines, one above the other
like surf coming in, like music.

2.
Your sand hills are clean and hard
and upright like young maidens.
Barrano is full of moonlight tonight,
the sweetness of white pear trees
as stifling as held breath. Onions are sprouting,
bees humming, and the apricots
wear frills of white lace. Time
and cottonwoods can't wait.

3.
First rays of sun in the dandelions.
Peaches straight from the trees, bright
with dew and sweet with August.

Look up at the sky and think of the star
riding along the mesa—the ranch
and the stillness and the stars.
So different from Texas where the air
is soft and grey and you forget the moon,
lock it in a closet. Different even
from Santa Fe, with its weight
of laughter and chatter.

4.
Deer leaping over the mountain,
golden with rain and sunlight.
Piedra Lumbre—*the burnt rock*—
and the little pink hill you painted,
curling into deep red brown, buttressed
by violet in the evening sun. Above
the western mesa, the evening star
hangs like a plum.

5.
No one can give yourself to yourself,
you told me once, and it's true.
But you gave yourself to me
in teaspoons, bittersweet
as fresh-squeezed lemon juice.

6.
You in a whang doodle of a mood,
climbing the clunky ladder in your plaid skirt
and wide-brimmed hat and plunking
your bony bottom down on the roof,
your smile a dare to anyone
who'd call your bluff.

7.
You on the patio in your metal lounger,
pen poised for your daily letter
to Alfred, your hair yanked back
in a pony tail, the cuffs of your khakis
deep enough to hold everything
I'll never have the pluck to say.

8.
The two of us in the garden,
you in a loose apron, me in a halter,
your hand on my bare shoulder
as I peel the carrots. The midday sun
allows no shadows, no secrets.

9.
Me in my faded Levi's, my hair
tied with a red ribbon, the top
of our mesa stored in my heart.

I believe in this world I see
from my window. I believe in skunks—
pintos: the painted ones—well-larded
with mallards under their ribs.
I believe in the gash of light
dividing summer and fall.
But perhaps this isn't enough.
Perhaps these words say nothing at all.

Notes

"Abridged" series: These erasure poems are comprised of words taken from the cited texts. The words are in order and have not been altered, with the exception of bracketed words, which have been added. The number of "erased" words between each selected word varies.

"Hand Mit Ringen": Wilhelm Rontgen discovered the x-ray in 1895. He and Anna were married forty-seven years until she died after a lengthy illness.

"Vienna Legends": Ignaz Seyfried was ten years old when he is said to have witnessed the meeting between Beethoven and Mozart in Vienna in 1787. Seyfried later studied under Mozart, and in 1805, he conducted the premiere of Beethoven's *Fidelio.*

"Alma Mahler, Postnuptial": The epigraph is an excerpt from a 20-page letter Gustav wrote to Alma in 1901, the year before they married. The letter specified his expectations and demands for their marriage, including the provision that Alma discontinue her own career in composition.

"Kant's Manservant": Reinhold Bernhard Jachmann was Kant's former student and friend who wrote an early biography of Kant.

"Nietzsche's Sister": Elisabeth Förster-Nietzsche was the younger sister of Friedrich Nietzsche. They were close as children but grew apart after she married the fanatic anti-Semite Bernhard Förster.

"Serving Schopenhauer": Arthur Schopenhauer's mother, Joanna Schopenhauer, is said to have tried to kill her son by pushing him down the stairs when he was a child.

"Basho's Disciple Challenges the Master": Japanese poet Matsuo Basho (1644-1694) is known for his *haikai no renga*, a collaborative form of linked poetry in which the opening 5-7-5 hokku is followed by a 7-7 verse by another poet.

"The Other Daughter": The speaker of this poem is Mary Wollstonecraft's first daughter, Fanny, who committed suicide at age 22. Wollstonecraft died following the birth of her second daughter, Mary, who went on to marry Percy Bysshe Shelley and to write *Frankenstein*. Among Wollstonecraft's writings is a collection of lessons on child care, from which the italicized lines in this poem are taken.

"The Fall": The epigraph is from a June 1851 letter to Emerson's brother, William, written after their mother, age 83, fell from her bed and broke her hip.

"The Lost Letter": Aunt Lavinia Norcross cared for Emily at age 2, while Emily's mother recovered from the birth of her second daughter, Lavinia "Vinnie" Dickinson.

"Poe's Last Letter, Abridged": Maria "Muddy" Clemm was Poe's aunt and mother-in-law. This letter, written on Sept. 18, 1849, is one of two letters written on that date. It is unclear which of the two is actually Poe's final correspondence.

"The Pantomime's Progeny": After Jean-Gaspard's death, his son Charles assumed the role of Pierrot with less success.

"Gutenberg's Verdict, Abridged": "The Helmasperger Notarial Instrument" was a 1455 document that recorded the findings of a court case in which Johannes Gutenberg was accused for misusing funds he had borrowed for his first printing press project. As a result of the verdict, he went bankrupt and lost his workshop, his equipment, and the naming rights to the Bible he had printed.

"To Nellie, with Love from the Letter E": The epigraph is from Brisbane's 1922 obituary for Cochrane. She was born Elizabeth Cochran but changed the spelling to "Cochrane" because she thought it seemed more sophisticated.

"Calamity Jane at the Dime Museum": "Calamity Jane" was a featured attraction at the Kohl & Middleton Dime Museum for six weeks in 1896.

"Emma Lazarus's Statue of Liberty Sonnet, Abridged": Lazarus's poem "The New Colossus" contains the famous lines "Give me your tired, your poor,/Your huddled masses yearning to breathe free..."

"Pluck and Jive": Flournoy Miller was part of the minstrel duo Miller and Lyles. In 1930, they sued Amos and Andy for using their material without providing credit or compensation. The "Amos and Andy" show ultimately hired Miller as a "consultant."

"Archimedes' Widow": Archimedes reportedly spoke these words just before he was killed by a Roman soldier during the Second Punic War, c. 212 B.C. Though myths abound about his wife "Marie," there is no definitive record of his having been married.

"Galileo's *Sidereal Messenger*, Abridged": *The Sidereal Messenger* (*Sidereus Nuncius*) is a treatise in which Galileo details his observations using a telescope.

"Mother of Invention": Tesla's older brother, Dane (pronounced "Dahnay"), died after being thrown from a horse. Tesla is thought to have suffered from synesthesia.

"The Causticity Principle": Pauli frequently expressed his disapproval of the work habits of Heisenberg, who first outlined his Uncertainty Principle in a fourteen-page letter to Pauli.

“Facing Manet”: Alexandre was a teenage boy who ran errands for Manet and posed for his painting “Boy with Cherries.” He hanged himself in Manet’s studio.

“Love Poem to Michelangelo”: Vittoria Colonna (1490-1547) was a confidante of Michelangelo and the subject of many of his drawings and poems.

“Letter from Van Gogh to Émile Bernard, Abridged”: Émile Bernard (1868-1941) was a fellow artist and friend of Van Gogh.

“Origen de Las Dos Fridas”: Frida Kahlo’s 1939 painting “Las Dos Fridas” (“The Two Fridas”) is a self-portrait portraying herself with contrasting personalities. She traced the idea for the painting to her memory of her childhood imaginary friend.

“Postcards from Ghost Ranch”: Chabot, who worked as a caretaker in exchange for room and board, was somewhat infatuated with O’Keefe. In their nearly decade-long correspondence—much of which focused on mundane information about home repairs, renovations, and bills—Chabot included occasional descriptions of the landscape. Some of the images in the poem are based on her descriptions.

www.ingramcontent.com/pod-product-compliance
Lightning Source LLC
Chambersburg PA
CBHW020947090426
42736CB00010B/1307
9780985083854